WILDLIFE VIEWING AREAS

Connecticut Ecoregions

- ■ Northeastern Highlands
- □ Northeastern Coastal Zone

- 1. Sharon Audubon Center
- 2. Housatonic Meadows State Park
- 3. Talcott Mountain State Park
- 4. Stamford Museum & Nature Center
- 5. Nipmuck State Forest/ Bigelow Hollow State Park
- 6. Connecticut State Museum of Natural History
- 7. Hartford Botanical Garden
- 8. Bluff Point State Park
- 9. Denison Pequotsepos Nature Center
- 10. Higby Mountain Preserve
- 11. Devil's Hopyard State Park

- 12. Hammonasset Beach State Park
- 13. East Rock Park/Trowbridge Environmental Center
- 14. Connecticut Audubon Society at Larsen Sanctuary
- 15. Sherwood Island State Park
- 16. Peabody Museum of Natural History
- 17. Audubon Center of Greenwich
- 18. Devil's Den Preserve
- 19. Bartlett Arboretum & Gardens
- 20. Earthplace, The Nature Discovery Center
- 21. Flanders Nature Center & Land Trust
- 22. White Memorial Conservation Center
- 23. Sessions Woods Wildlife Management Area

Waterford Press produces reference guides that introduce novices to nature, science, survival and outdoor recreation. Product information is featured on the website: www.waterfordpress.com

Text and illustrations © 2010, 2021 by Waterford Press Inc. All rights reserved. Cover images © Shutterstock. Ecoregion map © The National Atlas of the United States. To order, call 800-434-2555. For permissions, or to share comments, e-mail editor@waterfordpress.com. For information on custom-published products, call 800-434-2555 or e-mail info@waterfordpress.com.

ISBN 978-1-58355-612-2
$7.95 U.S.
Made in the USA

50795

9 781583 556122

8 84682 00948 9
UPC

10 9 8 7 6 5 4 3 2 1   210903

CONNECTICUT WILDLIFE – A Folding Pocket Guide to Familiar Animals

Kavanagh/Leung

A POCKET NATURALIST® GUIDE

CONNECTICUT WILDLIFE

A Folding Pocket Guide to Familiar Animals

T0123991

SEASHORE LIFE

Common Sea Star
Asterias forbesi
To 10 in. (13 cm)
May be tan, brown, orange or olive with orange highlights.

Spiny Sun Star
Crossaster papposus
To 14 in. (35 cm)

Frilled Anemone
Metridium senile
To 18 in. (45 cm)

Soft-shelled Clam
Mya arenaria
To 6 in. (15 cm)

Blood Star
Henricia sanguinolenta
To 4 in. (10 cm)

Eastern Oyster
Crassostrea virginica
To 10 in. (25 cm)
Connecticut's state shellfish.

Atlantic Bay Scallop
Argopecten irradians
To 3 in. (8 cm)

Blue Mussel
Mytilus edulis
To 4 in. (10 cm)
Grows attached to pilings and other marine objects.

Knobbed Whelk
Busycon carica
To 9 in. (23 cm)
Note prominent knobs on spire.

Common Periwinkle
Littorina littorea
To 1 in. (3 cm)

Northern Quahog
Mercenaria mercenaria
To 5 in. (13 cm)
Found in mud near low tide mark.

Fiddler Crab
Uca spp.
To 1.5 in. (4 cm)

Hermit Crab
Pagurus spp.
To 1.3 in. (3.6 cm)
Lives in discarded shells.

Northern Moon Snail
Lunatia heros
To 4.5 in. (11 cm)

Blue Crab
Callinectes sapidus
To 9 in. (23 cm)

Horseshoe Crab
Limulus polyphemus
To 12 in. (30 cm) wide

BUTTERFLIES

Eastern Tiger Swallowtail
Papilio glaucus
To 6 in. (15 cm)

Cabbage White
Pieris rapae
To 2 in. (5 cm)
One of the most common butterflies.

Spicebush Swallowtail
Papilio troilus
To 4.5 in. (11 cm)

Orange Sulphur
Colias eurytheme
To 2.5 in. (6 cm)

American Copper
Lycaena phlaeas
To 1.25 in. (3.2 cm)

Spring Azure
Celastrina ladon
To 1.3 in. (3.6 cm)
One of the earliest spring butterflies.

Silver-bordered Fritillary
Boloria selene
To 2 in. (5 cm)

Question Mark
Polygonia interrogationis
To 2.5 in. (6 cm)
Silvery mark on underwings resembles a question mark or semicolon.

Mourning Cloak
Nymphalis antiopa
To 3.5 in. (9 cm)

Red Admiral
Vanessa atalanta
To 2.5 in. (6 cm)

Baltimore Checkerspot
Euphydryas phaeton
To 2.5 in. (6 cm)

Monarch
Danaus plexippus
To 4 in. (10 cm)

Viceroy
Limenitis archippus
To 3 in. (8 cm)
Told from similar monarch by its smaller size and the thin, black band on its hindwings.

Red-spotted Purple
Limenitis arthemis astyanax
To 3.5 in. (9 cm)

White Admiral
Limenitis arthemis arthemis
To 3 in. (8 cm)
Common in upland deciduous forests.

REPTILES & AMPHIBIANS

Eastern Newt
Notophthalmus viridescens To 6 in. (15 cm)
Juvenile form – called a red eft – is red-orange.

Red Eft

Yellow-Spotted Salamander
Ambystoma maculatum
To 10 in. (25 cm)

American Toad
Anaxyrus americanus
To 4.5 in. (11 cm)

Spring Peeper
Pseudacris crucifer
To 1.5 in. (4 cm)
Musical call is a series of short peeps.

Gray Treefrog
Hyla versicolor
To 2.5 in. (6 cm)
Call is a strong, resonating trill.

Bullfrog
Lithobates catesbeianus
To 8 in. (20 cm)
Call is a deep-pitched – jug-o-rum.

Eastern Painted Turtle
Chrysemys picta picta
To 10 in. (25 cm)

Snapping Turtle
Chelydra serpentina To 18 in. (45 cm)
Note knobby shell and long tail.

Spotted Turtle
Clemmys guttata To 5 in. (13 cm)
Dark shell is yellow-spotted.

Eastern Box Turtle
Terrapene carolina carolina
To 9 in. (23 cm)

Northern Water Snake
Nerodia sipedon To 4.5 ft. (1.4 m)
Note dark blotches on back.

Northern Black Racer
Coluber constrictor
To 6 ft. (1.8 m)

Milk Snake
Lampropeltis triangulum
To 7 ft. (2.1 m)

Timber Rattlesnake
Crotalus horridus To 6 ft. (1.8 m)

Northern Ringneck Snake
Diadophis punctatus To 30 in. (75 cm)

GAME FISHES

American Shad
Alosa sapidissima To 30 in. (75 cm)
Note line of spots behind gill cover.
Connecticut's state fish.

Bluegill
Lepomis macrochirus To 16 in. (40 cm)

Largemouth Bass
Micropterus salmoides To 40 in. (1 m)
Jaw joint extends beyond the eye.

Black Crappie
Pomoxis nigromaculatus
To 16 in. (40 cm)

Yellow Perch
Perca flavescens To 16 in. (40 cm)
Note 6-9 dark "saddles" down its side.

Pumpkinseed
Lepomis gibbosus To 16 in. (40 cm)

Brook Trout
Salvelinus fontinalis To 28 in. (70 cm)
Reddish side spots have blue halos.

Landlocked Salmon
Salmo salar To 4.5 ft. (1.4 m)
Freshwater version of Atlantic salmon is brown-bronze colored.

Brown Trout
Salmo trutta To 40 in. (1 m)
Has red and black spots on its body.

Rainbow Trout
Oncorhynchus mykiss To 44 in. (1.1 m)
Note reddish side stripe.

Brown Bullhead
Ameiurus nebulosus To 20 in. (50 cm)
Brown above, white below with mottled sides.

Chain Pickerel
Esox niger To 31 in. (78 cm)
Has chain-like pattern on sides. Anadromous.

Bluefish
Pomatomus saltatrix To 43 in. (1.1 m)
Short first dorsal fin has 7-8 spines.

Striped Bass
Morone saxatilis To 6 ft. (1.8 m)
Has 6-9 dark side stripes.

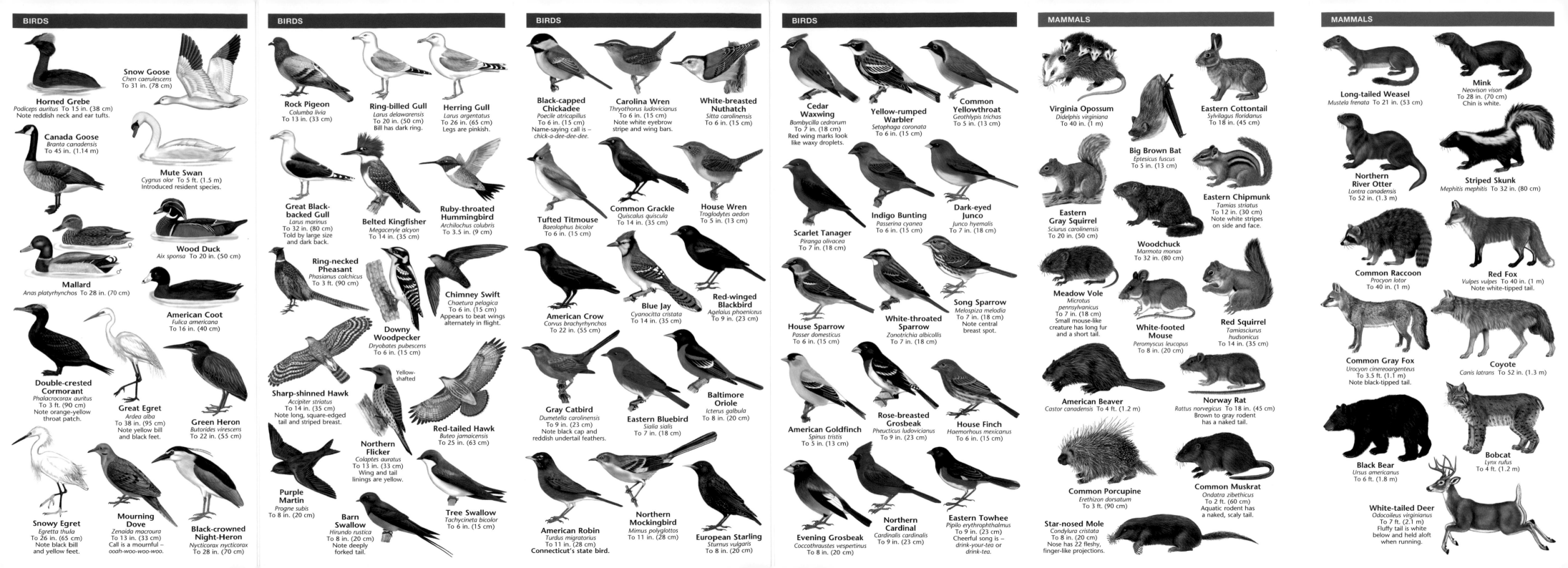

BIRDS

Horned Grebe
Podiceps auritus To 15 in. (38 cm)
Note reddish neck and ear tufts.

Snow Goose
Chen caerulescens
To 31 in. (78 cm)

Canada Goose
Branta canadensis
To 45 in. (1.14 m)

Mute Swan
Cygnus olor To 5 ft. (1.5 m)
Introduced resident species.

Wood Duck
Aix sponsa To 20 in. (50 cm)

Mallard
Anas platyrhynchos To 28 in. (70 cm)

American Coot
Fulica americana
To 16 in. (40 cm)

Double-crested Cormorant
Phalacrocorax auritus
To 3 ft. (90 cm)
Note orange-yellow
throat patch.

Great Egret
Ardea alba
To 38 in. (95 cm)

Green Heron
Butorides virescens
To 22 in. (55 cm)

Snowy Egret
Egretta thula
To 26 in. (65 cm)
Note black bill
and yellow feet.

Mourning Dove
Zenaida macroura
To 13 in. (33 cm)
Call is a mournful –
ooah-woo-woo-woo.

Black-crowned Night-Heron
Nycticorax nycticorax
To 28 in. (70 cm)

BIRDS

Rock Pigeon
Columba livia
To 13 in. (33 cm)

Ring-billed Gull
Larus delawarensis
To 20 in. (50 cm)
Bill has dark ring.

Herring Gull
Larus argentatus
To 26 in. (65 cm)
Legs are pinkish.

Great Black-backed Gull
Larus marinus
To 32 in. (80 cm)
Told by large size
and dark back.

Belted Kingfisher
Megaceryle alcyon
To 14 in. (35 cm)

Ruby-throated Hummingbird
Archilochus colubris
To 3.5 in. (9 cm)

Ring-necked Pheasant
Phasianus colchicus
To 3 ft. (90 cm)

Chimney Swift
Chaetura pelagica
To 6 in. (15 cm)
Appears to beat wings
alternately in flight.

Downy Woodpecker
Dryobates pubescens
To 6 in. (15 cm)

Sharp-shinned Hawk
Accipiter striatus
To 14 in. (35 cm)
Note long, square-edged
tail and striped breast.

Yellow-shafted

Northern Flicker
Colaptes auratus
To 13 in. (33 cm)
Wing and tail
linings are yellow.

Red-tailed Hawk
Buteo jamaicensis
To 25 in. (63 cm)

Purple Martin
Progne subis
To 8 in. (20 cm)

Barn Swallow
Hirundo rustica
To 8 in. (20 cm)
Note deeply
forked tail.

Tree Swallow
Tachycineta bicolor
To 6 in. (15 cm)

BIRDS

Black-capped Chickadee
Poecile atricapillus
To 6 in. (15 cm)
Name-saying call is –
chick-a-dee-dee-dee.

Carolina Wren
Thryothorus ludovicianus
To 6 in. (15 cm)
Note white eyebrow
stripe and wing bars.

White-breasted Nuthatch
Sitta carolinensis
To 6 in. (15 cm)

Tufted Titmouse
Baeolophus bicolor
To 6 in. (15 cm)

Common Grackle
Quiscalus quiscula
To 14 in. (35 cm)

House Wren
Troglodytes aedon
To 5 in. (13 cm)

American Crow
Corvus brachyrhynchos
To 22 in. (55 cm)

Blue Jay
Cyanocitta cristata
To 14 in. (35 cm)

Red-winged Blackbird
Agelaius phoeniceus
To 9 in. (23 cm)

Gray Catbird
Dumetella carolinensis
To 9 in. (23 cm)
Note black cap and
reddish undertail feathers.

Eastern Bluebird
Sialia sialis
To 7 in. (18 cm)

Baltimore Oriole
Icterus galbula
To 8 in. (20 cm)

American Robin
Turdus migratorius
To 11 in. (28 cm)
Connecticut's state bird.

Northern Mockingbird
Mimus polyglottos
To 11 in. (28 cm)

European Starling
Sturnus vulgaris
To 8 in. (20 cm)

BIRDS

Cedar Waxwing
Bombycilla cedrorum
To 7 in. (18 cm)
Red wing marks look
like waxy droplets.

Yellow-rumped Warbler
Setophaga coronata
To 6 in. (15 cm)

Common Yellowthroat
Geothlypis trichas
To 5 in. (13 cm)

Scarlet Tanager
Piranga olivacea
To 7 in. (18 cm)

Indigo Bunting
Passerina cyanea
To 6 in. (15 cm)

Dark-eyed Junco
Junco hyemalis
To 7 in. (18 cm)

House Sparrow
Passer domesticus
To 6 in. (15 cm)

White-throated Sparrow
Zonotrichia albicollis
To 7 in. (18 cm)

Song Sparrow
Melospiza melodia
To 7 in. (18 cm)
Note central
breast spot.

American Goldfinch
Spinus tristis
To 5 in. (13 cm)

Rose-breasted Grosbeak
Pheucticus ludovicianus
To 9 in. (23 cm)

House Finch
Haemorhous mexicanus
To 6 in. (15 cm)

Evening Grosbeak
Coccothraustes vespertinus
To 8 in. (20 cm)

Northern Cardinal
Cardinalis cardinalis
To 9 in. (23 cm)

Eastern Towhee
Pipilo erythrophthalmus
To 9 in. (23 cm)
Cheerful song is –
drink-your-tea or
drink-tea.

MAMMALS

Virginia Opossum
Didelphis virginiana
To 40 in. (1 m)

Eastern Cottontail
Sylvilagus floridanus
To 18 in. (45 cm)

Big Brown Bat
Eptesicus fuscus
To 5 in. (13 cm)

Eastern Gray Squirrel
Sciurus carolinensis
To 20 in. (50 cm)

Woodchuck
Marmota monax
To 32 in. (80 cm)

Eastern Chipmunk
Tamias striatus
To 12 in. (30 cm)
Note white stripes
on side and face.

Meadow Vole
Microtus pennsylvanicus
To 7 in. (18 cm)
Small mouse-like
creature has long fur
and a short tail.

White-footed Mouse
Peromyscus leucopus
To 8 in. (20 cm)

Red Squirrel
Tamiasciurus hudsonicus
To 14 in. (35 cm)

American Beaver
Castor canadensis
To 4 ft. (1.2 m)

Norway Rat
Rattus norvegicus To 18 in. (45 cm)
Brown to gray rodent
has a naked tail.

Common Porcupine
Erethizon dorsatum
To 3 ft. (90 cm)

Common Muskrat
Ondatra zibethicus
To 2 ft. (60 cm)
Aquatic rodent has a
naked, scaly tail.

Star-nosed Mole
Condylura cristata
To 8 in. (20 cm)
Nose has 22 fleshy,
finger-like projections.

MAMMALS

Long-tailed Weasel
Mustela frenata To 21 in. (53 cm)

Mink
Neovison vison
To 28 in. (70 cm)
Chin is white.

Northern River Otter
Lontra canadensis
To 52 in. (1.3 m)

Striped Skunk
Mephitis mephitis To 32 in. (80 cm)

Common Raccoon
Procyon lotor
To 40 in. (1 m)

Red Fox
Vulpes vulpes To 40 in. (1 m)
Note white-tipped tail.

Common Gray Fox
Urocyon cinereoargenteus
To 3.5 ft. (1.1 m)
Note black-tipped tail.

Coyote
Canis latrans To 52 in. (1.3 m)

Black Bear
Ursus americanus
To 6 ft. (1.8 m)

Bobcat
Lynx rufus
To 4 ft. (1.2 m)

White-tailed Deer
Odocoileus virginianus
To 7 ft. (2.1 m)
Fluffy tail is white
below and held aloft
when running.